I0159559

LETTERS
from
the End of Life

LETTERS
from
the End of Life

DAVID H. ROSEN

Foreword by René Good

RESOURCE *Publications* · Eugene, Oregon

LETTERS FROM THE END OF LIFE

Copyright © 2024 David H. Rosen. All rights reserved. Except for brief quotations in critical publications or reviews, no part of this book may be reproduced in any manner without prior written permission from the publisher. Write: Permissions, Wipf and Stock Publishers, 199 W. 8th Ave., Suite 3, Eugene, OR 97401.

Resource Publications
An Imprint of Wipf and Stock Publishers
199 W. 8th Ave., Suite 3
Eugene, OR 97401

www.wipfandstock.com

PAPERBACK ISBN: 979-8-3852-1807-3

VERSION NUMBER 051024

Contents

PART 3: FAMILY

Foreword

By René Good

It is my great honor to contribute to David Rosen's latest book, "Letters From The End Of Life". I have been blessed to have come to know David's intellect, his deep love for family and friends, thoughtfulness, sense of humor and his appreciation for all things great and small.

I have been a member of David's caregiving team during the past year. He has faced his tribulations due to MS and ensuing limitations with grace and dignity.

In "Reflections" David embraces his acceptance of "crossing over" as a natural part of our human existence and the inevitable final journey.

Letters to MS describe him nursing physical pain and the mental suffering due to the awareness of his body's deterioration. David's ability to seek a positive purpose during this time is commendable! His spirit and minds focus on learning, understanding and sharing this knowledge has been his life's purposeful journey.

Appreciation for those who have been awarded the gift of assisting David during this time shows his desire to leave his thanks in a heartfelt way.

David's phenomenal love for his family is known to all. Writing to each, his love of their awsome attributes and wishes for their future will be a positive guide for them.

I am sure David's powerful energy and love will be transfered into a positive spirit with an impact on all who have ever known him.

Peace & Gratitude

Acknowledgements

I want to thank the folks at the hospice house, here, in Eugene, Oregon for stimulating my thoughts about this worthwhile activity, which helped so many people who are crossing over. I want to thank equanimity for their assistance with this project. There's nothing like being balanced when trying to tackle something like this. These letters originally grew out of a stay that I had in a hospice facility. You'll note that in these descriptions I sat with dear hospice for a while before putting down these words. Enjoy.

Prelude

What an eye opener for me to enter Hospice. Hospice is provided for a person with a terminal illness whose doctor believes he or she has six months or less to live. So, you must be in the realm of dying, to enter. It sounds a bit morbid, but it is not. It is just a natural part of life. I like the Hospice staff because they are dedicated to helping you in an altruistic, holistic way and to provide comfort care when necessary. I thought many times of the nature of Hospice staff. They are responsible, devoted, attentive and willing to sit down and talk for as long as necessary. These dedicated soldiers of Hospice healing are committed to something so rare and precious that you wish there was much more of its kind in our society.

My Hospice intake was done by Rebecca. She did a thorough and sensitive interview and evaluation. Hospice has provided Lanara and me a lot of support and frequent visits. My first at-home Hospice nurse Rebe is sensitive, competent, spiritual, interesting, and kind. I was happy to learn she likes *"Women Who Run with the Wolves"* by Clarissa Pinkola Estes, a colleague and friend. Rebe's assistant, Reyanna, is a positive individual who feels called to do the work and has plans to become a Hospice nurse herself in the future.

Having a respite stay at the Pete Moore Hospice House was recommended by a Physical Therapist. So, I applied in December and was approved for five days, December 28, 2023 through January 2, 2024. This respite was not only for me but also for my wife, Lanara, who takes very good care of me daily. Pete Moore's legacy is a good one. It is a kind & altruistic gift that has made the end of life better for many people. Staying at that unique facility, even though it was only for five days, changed my perspective and has given me appreciation for what Pete built. This successful businessman has had a real and meaningful impact on many people's lives and deaths. He built it to last and to be of service to the Hospice community. It was his wonderful idea to have a unique place where people can go at the end of life, or have a respite from the stresses of everyday life, living with a serious illness.

It is like a home, with all the rooms you'd find in an old house or your grandmother's place. Every patient has their own room with a fireplace and a door to the outside patio and natural area. There is an exercise room, a library, a family room, and even a kitchen that is open to family members and guests. The grounds are nicely landscaped. The staff are kind and caring individuals, but just think of your last family get together, there's always a little bit of tension. It is hard work keeping the patients content and well fed and it seemed they didn't have adequate staff to support each patient's unique needs.

Our new year's eve celebration there was the best part of my stay. My daughters created a festive party atmosphere, decorating the room with silver streamers. We wore new year's eve headbands and necklaces, which Ember, who is pushing two years old, particularly loved.

We danced to good music. The staff joined in and was affected by the happiness. One was a middle-aged lady who made a comment about being a comedian. Then there was the elderly lady who was ripened to the fine degree of good cheer and good relationship. She loved to interact with us young people. I remember Thomas who would have to be called to help when I had to be moved. He had good cheer. Then there was Molly who would come in at the night shift. She had her long black hair curled and was very friendly. The place was crowded and the staff was always busy. One of the oddest experiences for me was feeling like I was back in my medical school years when I was on a ward by myself and I heard death rattles. I heard them from a man and woman and I knew exactly what they meant. Here I was at Hospice house a good five decades later. There is a unique sound that doctors can recognize in death rattles.

What I found was a kind and competent staff, but I quickly realized I'd rather be in my own house. The grounds were beautiful, but I knew that I'd prefer real nature where I live with my wife, Lanara. The gardens she planted are striking and beautiful. She's even included some trees, like persimmons, nectarine, and peach. Several times I quietly thanked Pete Moore for what he did as a legacy which was so significant in helping others during their end-of-life experience.

On reflection I personally went there too soon as I'm not dying like others who were staying there. I didn't need all the Hospice medicines they gave me and I wasn't able to leave my bed. I've never been more happy to be back home and it's taken me a while to recover from being away from home. That is the reason why I decided not to go back. Because I found everything here at home, and I'd rather be with Lanara than anyone else. My typist Nick also enjoys time with Lanara and me. Lanara likes, especially, his interests in environmentalism.

So now, what do I do with newfound time & energy? How could having MS relate to anything positive? That is easy to answer. I attribute writing over thirty books due to the stresses related to this illness. Writing is my stress release. Some people like to travel every year, I like to write a book every year—and I often will travel places in my books.

But writing is good for more than just people near the end, so why not have a new adolescence that will fulfill those promises? I say adolescence because it's a time when we're not afraid to try things.

Dear Hospice House,

Thank you for existing, although I wish it was for different things. It's important to begin to deal with one's sickness, illness, and of course death — so shouldn't it be that everyone gets a ticket to go to Hospice House? But, I'm sure if they were given away, people would not want to take them. What is it about death that drives people away? Why is this the case? Is this because Americans are terrified of old age, and they worship youth? Therefore, it seems obvious why Americans don't deal with this basic fact of life effectively.

Are the Zen monks correct? I was about to answer this question, but a hospice nurse walked in, so there was a slight delay. Back to the question. Are death and life the same? But how could they be the same, I mean, what about the profession of philosophy, and their multi-task to figure it out: Why are we here? What is this death stuff about? And do I have to go through it too?—I'm now an older man and ready to experience this foreign land. I've heard that when we stop racing cars we live longer. But, I want to race. We should reflect on this saying, why would it be wrong to be number two? To die with dignity first, or second, may not matter.

And what was going through James Dean's mind when he was racing towards death? Dean starred in *Rebel*

Without a Cause (1955), but he became a rebel with a cause. Dean realized he could do anything you want to, so long as you persist, and he gave that cause to many young people. He told young people that they were important, and could do things, even when others were saying the opposite. He was giving credibility to even non-athletic people in high schools. He was in between a normal person and a rebel, working his way up to having a cause. What individual with a limited acting career and ability wanted to be just like James Dean, and probably was? Elvis. But back to the question at hand: Life and death aren't the same, but they're pretty damn close.

PART 1

REFLECTIONS

Dear Death,

I am sorry to meet you in this unexpected way. I am not afraid, but I am fascinated by the subject of stepping into the shadows and entering this waning moon. Why is death so scary to people? Probably a simple answer, we'd rather stay alive, be alive.

However, I am ill with a chronic neurological condition called MS. Multiple Sclerosis, a disease in which the nerve sheaths are attacked, making one vulnerable to this disease. I just want to say that you have outdone yourself.

Dear MS,

MS forced me and others to face the fact that we are terminal. MS illuminates that this life is ending and pain and suffering are inevitable. Hence, it is better to focus on pain, suffering, depth and death, long before they happen. For this reason it may be a good idea to pick a grave site, or method of remembrance, before one actually dies. You can be remembered through your ashes, a burial tree, or even a memoir, which compliments what you've done in life.

The Hollywood presentation, or our culture's approach to death and dying, sometimes speeds up the dying process. For example, the overuse of sedation and medications such as morphine which could diminish the patient's ability to communicate, create, or discover meaning which are essential.

This is why I say thank you to MS. Most people don't see illness as a positive turn of events, but it is a part of you that needs your help and attention. A person who can find meaning in suffering, like in Victor Frankl's *Man's Search for Meaning*, is in a realm few inhabit.

MS has allowed me to slow down and value each creative moment. For it's not by accident that I would write more books during this time period than ever before. I am also not as controlling as I once was, and in both Jungian analysis and my writing, I am freer, more open, and think about things in a new way. I've noticed that it's now easier to write because I am less self-critical and self-loathing. Creating, being with and helping others, and spending time with family, are my new pastimes, and may be why MS has came to mean "Making Sense" to me. I've noticed in this a welcome change, with less focus on professional achievements. It is easier now to tell the truth. I don't care if I write something acclaimed, complex, or innovative. The inner self-critic is no longer in the driver's seat, and sometimes not even in the passenger's seat. It is just gone which is a gift.

Dear Pain,

I didn't know that you had teamed up with MS, but, "thank you." Why would I dare say "thank you"? Because it means I am alive.

To be in pain acknowledges that you're aware of pain and your experience of it. It is a fine line—you don't want to just eliminate it, but you do want to take the edge off of it to lessen the agony. But here's an interesting idea that I use: pain and frustration mean that I am alive and can grapple with other ideas, even writing another book that seems remarkable and unlikely, but possible.

If pain wasn't there you'd be in a worse off place. Why? Because I've learned that you're only alive if you have pain. When my leg aches and my left shoulder is hurting, I KNOW that I am alive! I know, also that the "Bug A Boo" MS is working on me. I didn't use to think of illness as a challenge related to growth. But it is and can be an important marker in your life.

In 2009, I came home from seeing Dr. Joan Jensen, a Neurologist, for my left arm, vision and leg problem causing trouble walking. When she told me I had MS, I almost fell off the exam table. She said, noting my reaction, "this is not a death sentence there are treatments". This is a complex illness. This is true there are treatments. Some general and some specific. First, you need to have regular injections of Copaxone (Glatiramer acetate), then there is another treatment, Ampyra (Dalfampridine) an oral medication. I was on these medications for many years until Joan said, "You do not need to take the injections anymore, just the oral tablet." I asked, "Why?" Her reply, "Because you do not have any new lesions." I was glad to hear that, but it was like a cardiac patient being told, "because you don't have new heart attacks". I was still disabled.

Dear Reader,

It's been a joy to finally meet you, because I've been a writer for most of my life. However, I've spent many years reading, and as it is commonly known, good writers are good readers. It's interesting and noteworthy, as to what I've been writing and reading, that death and rebirth commonly appear. When you put those two together, they tend to want to stay together. Rebirth is an opportunity to live again consciously. People often speak of the "afterlife," but I am interested in "afterdeath."

PART 2

APPRECIATION

Dear Hospice,

To the nurses at the Pete Moore Hospice House: there were several of you, and I thank you for your abilities and kindnesses. As for the food, it was no better no worse than any other institutional hospital. Why are you so mediocre? Is it because after building such a nice place, Pete Moore could not afford to hire gourmet cooks? I know you're in heaven, Pete, but I'm still going to send this to you by special delivery. I know you did such a good job with the Hospice House, but if you ever need to visit heaven again — or maybe you go away on vacation, and want to come back from Cuba — maybe you could do the same thing for the United States penal system. If people have to be in prison, why not give them rooms like those at the hospice house? Why not have a fireplace, nice facilities, and good food?

Pete, thank you for your altruistic vision. The creation of the Hospice House says a lot about you. What a legacy. And a meaningful act of kindness.

Dear Academia,

You are a complex entity, which I benefited from. Some of these unique benefits are: the best job in the world, good steady pay, and sabbaticals, which, tragically, most professors do not take. However, as far as I'm concerned, that's the best perk that exists. It worked out great in Switzerland, Japan, and New Zealand. I was in Switzerland for seven months because I combined my summer time with a semester's worth of sabbatical. I used this time to write the Tao of Jung, which has been spoken of by Laura London as a true achievement.

Dear Alex,

How are you?

This is a new experience. I was walking and going out to eat with you at various places. But I really just miss you and our conversations. I've known you for over 9 years and you used to help me 4 days a week. You used to help me write stuff. We'd just talk about whatever. I was very pleased and honored to be asked to be the celebrant at your wedding. June 29th,2024. So, thank you for that opportunity and I know we'll always stay in touch and not forget each other. When we were first together, we'd go in all those restaurants, like Sushi Domo, and they would ask if you were my son or grandson. That happens a lot. So, I think you were sent to me by God, so I could have a son. Also, you were open and very informally adopted, and we just want to ask your parents to get their consent.

Dear Nick,

How wonderful to have another student from the philosophy department to assist me with my writing. Thank you for bringing out the reality of my philosophy, onto the page. I feel blessed in that way.

Thank you for your help with my writing and having to put up with requests from Lanara right when you come in the door. But don't worry, this has been the usual for years. Alex can tell you that. On the positive side, it's great for someone new to help me with my creative ideas in typing and to make sure the ideas and plans that I think are good are actually fine.

Dear Kimberly,

Thanks, Kimberly, for always reminding me I have 6 more pills left. But, on the other side, you've been patient to hear and take in my raspy words and suggest that "those words could be less raspy if you did this. . .".

Dear Desiree,

Thank you for going above and beyond, braving the ice storm and power outages to be here with me.

Dear Desiree's Team,

We like all of you. Thank you for your help and kindness.

Dear James,

You know better than anyone that the Hospice House is a facility, but not a home. They call it the Pete Moore Hospice House, but in reality it is an institution with all the staff and rules that go with such a place. What a unique experience that I won't choose to do again. I would prefer to be in my own home. You were right about the Pete Moore House.

James, having gotten to know you, my appreciation for your services has deepened. You are strong and steady, which is critically handy in this profession as well as other activities. You are ethical, and open to new ideas. And if you were willing to put up with all the stress and strain of going to medical school, you would make an excellent physician.

PART 3

FAMILY

Dear Sarah Rosen-Garrett, daughter,

Thank you for coming to Hospice House on New Years Eve. What a fun and meaningful celebration, it was heart-warming to have you, Laura, and Rachel all there, as well as Ben, Ember, Lia and Paul, what a rare treat.

Now I am going to shift to a different topic that has blessed your life.

You've always been concerned about the environment. When you were young you encouraged teachers and students at your school to recycle and went door to door to people's houses and asked them to change their behavior, and not to throw horrible things in the trash. In College Station, Texas, in the 1980s, that was unusual. That was before schools and businesses recycled anything. That's an overwhelming problem that didn't stop you - you took it on. There was then a change in behavior, at your school, and in parts of the community, which is rare. . . Both are unusual. . . Typically, people just talk about change. You're what they call a mover and a shaker. You've always been aware and done your part. Being a young girl; and having awareness of environmental problems was unusual, but that's how you were, and how you are.

It's essential that we all take care of our planet—not just on Earth Day, but every day, and you've known that from a young age which is remarkable.

As a toddler, you always wanted to be carried so you could look out, and see where you were going, which is a trait that has served you well because you noticed where you are, and what's needed, and you've done well. You are aware of issues that need to be addressed and resolved, and you've not only thought about it, but you've done it.

Early on, asking Carolyn Fay for funding, and being told "No", caused you to dig deeper and find your own "Yes".—which is harder, but you did it. You asked her specifically, "Would you support the Hope School?" and her answer prompted your own growth and development. You turned a "No" into a "Yes" and relied on your own internal resources and others who helped you.

I remember you asking me, "How do you ask people to give money?" and I said "You just ask them" because each person who gets involved has had their own project or idea they wanted to realize, but didn't do it, and they got on your bandwagon, and they feel a part of it, because you have a good nature and have allowed people to be a part of something meaningful.

In childhood, it is interesting that your dedication to your projects took precedence in a lot of what you did, which is unusual for a child. I think kids think about ideas, and want to do that, but usually they don't and just let it go and go and play.

You wanted to look out as a toddler, and in your childhood and adolescence you wanted to do something that mattered which is a good attribute to have. Other people turn to sororities or partying, or some other bad habits, but the good news is that all that can be turned around. Just let yourself out of your own prison and let yourself do what you've always wanted to do. Sounds too easy, but it's difficult, as you know.

So why not have letters to the future things you want to do . . . Why aren't there classes in elementary, junior high and high school that are devoted to the dreams that people have. school outlining dreams students would like to develop.

You have to give yourself credit. It is unusual to notice what's wrong and come up with a system or idea to change it, and then to do it, so you are in an exceptional group. It is very unique for an individual to do that on their own, which sets you apart in many ways, and allows you to inspire others through your example.

You can do anything you want now because you've already done it. There was a time I thought it wouldn't be possible to write a book, but then I went to a writers workshop, and after that, I didn't have to ask, are you a writer? . . . I just knew I was. . . I didn't know I could do that, but I could . . . Most people don't know they can do something that was once a dream, but you know you can, which gives you a fuller and more meaningful view of life.

You had an awakening early on that you could realize your dreams which is uncommon.

So in closing, you are a special person with vision which I applaud. I am so proud of you and all you have accomplished.

Love,
Dad

Dear Rachel,

From the time that you were born in Strong Memorial Hospital in Rochester, New York, you have been an energetic, gung-ho, I-know-what-I-want-to-do individual. At times this was scary when you fell down the steps, but you didn't hurt yourself. At other times it led you to touch base with Graceland through your teddy-bear. We used to have moon walks around the neighborhood, and you were always struck by how the moon knew to follow us. I had the same reaction. Your desire to play basketball was rewarded by enthusiastic joining in shooting matches like Horse. And on your team with the police chief's wife when I was the assistant coach of your junior high basketball team. On that team, you were a forceful and excellent team player. I think in your bravado you even tried out for and played on a flag football team. It's interesting that in Salem, Oregon they have women's professional tackle football.

What would you say the highlights were of your schooling? I was impressed with your performance in public school and your special projects as you outlined which ones you had the most affinity for. We both like to write so we chose books and we liked to read together. You would say "I like that book." Also your bravery was exhibited in Japan when you played your cello with Hayo

Kawaii at this huge Japanese auditorium. I don't think you'd ever seen that music before. I think it was Mendelssohn. You played it accurately and gracefully. After the performance we went back to his office. He was the head of a Japanese research institute and had a cook who prepared a meal for us. Both Kawaii and I said "fresh! Enjoy". They love raw fish. So you ate it. It had rice and some kind of vegetable—I can't remember what it was. When Hayo Kawaii came to College Station to give the Fay Lectures on Buddhism and the Art of Psychotherapy he wanted to make sure that you would be there. You came to one of his Fay Lectures and the dinner, which were always exceptional.

You always had a propensity for story-telling. When we would go for moon walks, I would ask you about the different characters and what was happening in the story, and we'd pick up exactly where you left off. You are a really good writer. If you decide to break out and ever write a novel, it would be good. And you have such a wide interest in various subjects, and memoir would be exciting because of your unique and dynamic life. You are a good mother and I really like Ember. I think you and Lia have done a marvelous job raising Ember.

You're so young. You only just turned 40, but you'll cross the mid-life red line in the sand soon. Between 40 and 70 are the most productive years available to anyone. I never would have thought I'd write 30 books by the time I was my age, and I am not braggin! I really did it. My father's father, "Pop" or Abraham, once told me on the porch swing in Springfield Missouri, "the best years of your life are way ahead of you. You can't even imagine. 70–90 are the best years". I would say it differently. The best years are between 40–80, but I'm open. Maybe Pop was right.

Other unique characteristics that you possess are an openness to all experiences. You're open to many possibilities. Being open to all experiences can be modeled to your kids. It's difficult to combine athletic and intellectual things, but you have a history of doing it, and that would be important for Ember because she'll have a different model in the mothers and families that she meets and visits. I think you have the insight. You'll develop your streams of creativity which most people talk about as missed opportunities. Don't do that. Follow the streams of creativity and travel. There's no better way to learn about other experiences than travel, because it introduces you to different languages, cultures, and fascinating ways of life.

At any rate, keep enjoying your life and your lovely family. I'm blessed to know and love Ember, you, and Lia.

In closing, the bottom line and critical aspect of an exciting life is to know yourself and accept yourself, and then you can extend yourself. So if you're invited to go to China, go. If it's possible to check out Korea—south or north—do it. And if an urgent originally unplanned side-trip to northern India is given to you, with maps and keys for your rental car—take it.

Love,
Dad
PS- have fun

Dear Laura,

You are my California girl. Born in Berkeley. Smart as a Berkeley student. Berkeley was a special place. We lived in a little bungalow with a small backyard and garden. 713 Spruce Street. It turned out to be a good investment. That's how we bought the houses in New York and College Station. From the deck in front of the house you could see the Golden Gate Bridge. We also had a little garden in the back. We even grew artichokes. This was a special house. Almost like a fairy tale. That was your baby home. I wonder what your first memories are. We were all thrilled about your arriving on the scene. Sarah welcomed you, learning quickly that she was no longer an only child. I've always been impressed by how close all three of you are with each other. You were always the thoughtful, serious, and happy child. Very curious about everything, which is still true. Then out of your experience you developed a strength, which still serves you well. You also have always stood up for what you believe.

We both have love of travel and I've gotten to share adventures with you in the places you've lived abroad. I'll never forget our time in Peru at Machu Picchu. What an honor to get the Fulbright Scholarship in Peru to conduct research on microfinance in Cusco. I went there and you showed me around the town and its old carved ceremonial stones and the beautiful city that was the capital of Peru at one time. We had a lovely Peruvian dinner with an American Fulbright friend. Going there was an exciting adventure. We had to take a traditional single-track train, uniquely furnished, like it used to be in the old days. It took us from Cusco to Machu Picchu. Thank you for opening the door for me to go to Peru because I'd always wanted to go there. I remember we stayed in Sanctuary Lodge that was recommended by Shirley MacLaine in her book about Machu Picchu. It was a movie star place with special rooms, accommodations, and food. From our breakfast on the front veranda, we could see Machu Picchu in front of us. Because we were guests there, we got to enter before the first tourists arrived in buses. Because it's such a special place, this has become one of the leading tourist attractions in the world. Still it would be worthwhile to go there because it has a unique history and majestic beauty. It's such an adventurous and dramatic place. You feel like you're part of the mountains and the clouds. Like you might be a condor.

Like myself you've always been a serious student. On the side of study rather than party, so I remember you in your room working on problems instead of being out galivanting around, and that has set a standard for your life. You were accepted as an honors student at UT Austin, which is a major accomplishment, and I want everyone to know.

However, in addition to your strengths as a student, you are a delightful person who is altruistic and caring. And as you know those traits are integral to positive relationships, and a meaningful life, and myself, Lanara, and your dear sisters, are extremely thankful for your presence on this Earth. Always remember your dreams, both day and night, because they can come true.

I'm very proud of your special work at Dell Medical School, which links us together in a meaningful way. We both have been in academia and teachers and have similar personalities with a special place in our hearts for students. You can't teach without knowing something. We both love teaching and mentoring students.

Also, you don't realize that you're a very good writer and when you do, you'll have books that will fly off the shelf. You'll always have a special place in my heart.

Love,
Dad

Dear Aidan,

I've watched you grow up over the years and maintain your interest in film, and I wish you all the best in that area of your interests and expertise. You have always been smart, creative, and playful, and we enjoyed having you stay with us at our house on Floral Hill Drive. You liked to go upstairs in the study and draw and play, and I wondered if you were mirroring me because I do too much of that myself. I remember your fondness for nature, and I recall once on a walk that you said that the leaves were like rattles making music. No matter what you do, you'll bring a creative edge to your work and clearly succeed in your finest ambitions.

Love,
Pop

Dear Ben,

I hope you're thriving down there in San Antonio. Why wouldn't you? It's such a great city. I remember when you were a boy and open to all kinds of foods—I bet you're eating at some good restaurants down there! You've always wanted to be a businessperson, so you'll do well in that area. You have always been an extroverted and friendly person. Being kind to people will always serve you in life and will help you with whatever vocation you settle on. No matter what you do, your discipline and varied interests will take you great places.

    Love,

    Pop

Dear Ember,

I have fond memories of you as a baby and as a young toddler. You have always been so free-spirited with your art. I know it will continue to liberate you. Weren't we lucky to have such artistic and talented parents? They supported and encouraged all creative efforts, which was and is a godsend. One of my favorite moments was New Years Eve 2023. You won't remember, but you were the light of the party, dancing and singing and bringing joy. Everybody young and old celebrated your feelings. And you weren't even two years old! No matter what you do in life, utilize your creative abilities and talents of which you have many. Just know that your grandfather was always impressed with what you talked about, painted, and wrote about.

Love, Pop

Dear Lanara,

How could I write such a letter concerning one of us losing the other one? I guess it's called reality-therapy. In other words, we live full lives, and that's what we're going to write about and deal with. Except, that both of us know there's something else after this life—the afterlife (or "afterdeath"). Isn't the real reason why we're all so concerned about being alone that we've forgotten about how comforting that state is? Alone is really "all one."

At least I know
that you have never forgotten
afterlife and afterdeath

You are one of the most gracious, generous, and glorious individuals that I've ever known. So, I'm confident that you'll keep living after dying. I feel honored to have known, loved, and married you. So I know about the depth of your feelings and beliefs, and they are true. Having almost reached the summit of Mount Eighty, I realize that the view from there will be one of a kind. And if I'm not with you, I will be with you soon.

P.S. If you want to drop this in the nearest mailbox of the heart, don't forget to address it first. I'll be looking forward to receiving it.

www.ingramcontent.com/pod-product-compliance
Lightning Source LLC
Chambersburg PA
CBHW060630030426
42337CB00018B/3288